WRIGHT FAMILY DEATH RECORDS (1853-1920)
CEMETERY RECORDS BY CEMETERY AND
PROBATE RECORDS (1782-1900)
IN
CAMPBELL COUNTY, VIRGINIA

Robert N. Grant

HERITAGE BOOKS
2011

HERITAGE BOOKS
AN IMPRINT OF HERITAGE BOOKS, INC.

Books, CDs, and more—Worldwide

For our listing of thousands of titles see our website
at
www.HeritageBooks.com

Published 2011 by
HERITAGE BOOKS, INC.
Publishing Division
100 Railroad Ave. #104
Westminster, Maryland 21157

International Standard Book Numbers
Paperbound: 978-0-7884-3810-3
Clothbound: 978-0-7884-8785-9

WRIGHT FAMILY

DEATH RECORDS

CAMPBELL COUNTY, VIRGINIA

1853 to 1920

Revised as of September 19, 2004

Introduction To Appendix: Death Records for Campbell County, Virginia

This document is an appendix to a larger work titled Sorting Some Of The Wrights Of Southern Virginia. The work is divided into parts for each family of Wrights that has been researched. Each part is divided into two sections; the first section is text discussing the family and the evidence supporting the relationships and the second section is a descendants chart summarizing the relationships and information known about each individual.

The appendices to the work (of which this document is one) present source records for persons named Wright by county and by type of record with the identification of the person named and their Wright ancestors to the extent known.

The source for the records listed in this appendix is the following:

1) Campbell County, Virginia, Death Records, available from the Commonwealth of Virginia, Department of Health, Division of Vital Records, P.O. Box 1000, Richmond, Virginia 23208-1000.

The identification of a person or their ancestor by year and county indicates their year of death and county of residence at death. For example, "1763 Thomas Wright of Bedford County" indicates that this was the Thomas Wright who died in 1763 in Bedford County. If no state is listed after the county, the state is Virginia; counties in states other than Virginia will have a state listed after the county, as in "1876 William S. Wright of Highland County, Ohio".

A parenthetical after the name indicates an identification of the person when a place of death is not yet known, as in "John Wright (Goochland County Carpenter)". A county in parentheses after the name indicates the county with which that person was most identified when no evidence of the place of death has yet been found, as in "Grief Wright (Bedford County)".

All or portions of the text and descendants charts for each Wright family identified are available from the author:

Robert N. Grant
15 Campo Bello Court   (H) 650-854-0895
Menlo Park, California 94025   (O) 650-614-3800

This is a work in progress and I would be most interested in receiving additional information about any of the persons identified in these records in order to correct any errors or expand on the information given.

Appendix: Campbell County, Virginia Index of Death Records

Book/Page	Date	Decedent	Information	Identification
	1855/08/19	Judith W. Wright	Place of Death: Campbell or Appomattox County Race: White Sex: Female Age: 26 Cause: Tumor Parents: Tho. & C. Gannaway Consort of: Wm. P. Wright Informant: Wm. P. Wright Relation of Informant: Husband	Probably Judith A. (Walden) Wright, wife of 1910 William P. Wright of Appomattox County, a son of Daniel P. Wright, grandson of 1811 John Wright of Campbell County, and probably great grandson of Robert Wright, Sr., (Campbell County)
	1864/10/25	Mollie Wright	Place of Death: Campbell County Race: White Sex: Female Age: 14 Cause: Typhoid Fever Parents: Thom & M. Wright Born: Campbell Informant: Tho. S. Wright Relation of Informant: Father	Mary "Mollie" S. Wright, daughter of 1883 Thomas S. Wright of Campbell County and granddaughter of 1842 Thomas Wright of Buckingham County
	1872/07/11	Cinderella Wright	Place of Death: Campbell County Race: White Sex: Female Age: 3 yrs, 6 mos & 5 days Cause: Fever Parents: Silas & Ann Wright Born: Campbell Consort of: Unmarried Informant: Silas Wright Relation of Informant: Head of Family	

Appendix: Campbell County, Virginia Index of Death Records

Book/Page	Date	Decedent	Information	Identification
	1874/07/15	Fannie Wright	Place of Death: Campbell County Race: Colored Sex: Female Age: 57 Born: Campbell Informant: P. P. Yuille Relation of Informant: Employer	
	1874/10/17	S. R. Wright	Place of Death: Campbell County Race: White Sex: Male Age: 9 mos Cause: Infant Parents: S. & L. Wright Born: Campbell Occupation: Laborer Consort of: Robt. Wright Informant: L. Wright Relation of Informant: Mother	1874 S. R. Wright of Campbell County, probably son of 1884 Sterling Charles Wright of Campbell County, grandson of 1873 Robert D. Wright of Amherst County, great grandson of Charles Wright, and great great grandson of Robert Wright, Sr., (Campbell County)
	1874/11/19	Mathilda Wright	Place of Death: Campbell County Race: White Sex: Female Age: 25 Cause: Childbirth Born: Campbell Informant: T. B. Wright Relation of Informant: Father-in-Law	Matilda C. (Hendrick) Wright, wife of James Robert Wright of Campbell County, a son of 1882 Thomas B. Wright of Campbell County and grandson of Thomas Wright (Campbell County)

Appendix: Campbell County, Virginia Index of Death Records

Book/Page	Date	Decedent	Information	Identification
	1876/01/05	Phillip Wright	Place of Death: Campbell County Race: Colored Sex: Male Age: 76 Cause: Disease of Stomach Born: Campbell Occupation: Farmer Informant: Dr. Thos. E. Moorman Relation of Informant: Friend	
	1879/07/05	Lucie Wright	Place of Death: Campbell County Race: Colored Sex: Female Age: 105 Informant: Thos. S. Wright Relation of Informant: Friend	
	1879/10/20	____ Wright	Place of Death: Campbell County Race: White Sex: Female Age: 2 mos Parents: Wm. R. & Christina W. Wright Informant: Wm. R. Wright Relation of Informant: Father	Daughter of William R. Wright, granddaughter of 1882 Thomas B. Wright of Campbell County, and great granddaughter of Thomas Wright (Campbell County)
	1880/05/22	Elijah Wright	Place of Death: Campbell County Race: White Sex: Male Age: 80 Place: Campbell County Cause: Heart Disease Born: Bedford County Consort of: Widower Informant: Saml Woodall Relation of Informant: Neighbor	1880 Elijah Wright of Campbell County, son of 1835 Benjamin Wright of Bedford County, grandson of 1814 John Wright of Bedford County, and great grandson of John Wright (Goochland County Carpenter)

Appendix: Campbell County, Virginia Index of Death Records

Book/Page	Date	Decedent	Information	Identification
	1882/01/01	Tho. B. Wright	Place of Death: Campbell County Race: White Sex: Male Age: 67 Cause: Pneumonia Parents: Tho. & Susan Wright Born: Campbell County Occupation: Farmer Consort of: Nancy Wright Informant: N. Wright Relation of Informant: Wife	1882 Thomas B. Wright of Campbell County, son of Thomas Wright (Campbell County)
	1882/11/24	Eliza Wright	Place of Death: Campbell County Race: White Sex: Female Age: 32 Cause: Consumption Parents: Tho. & Nancy Wright Born: Campbell Occupation: Domestic Affairs Consort of: Unmarried Informant: N. Wright Relation of Informant: Mother	Eliza Wright, daughter of 1882 Thomas B. Wright of Campbell County and granddaughter of Thomas Wright (Campbell County)
	1883/04/30	Alice R. Wright	Place of Death: Campbell County Race: Colored Sex: Female Age: 14 Cause: Rheumatism Parents: Nelson & Sarah Wright Born: Campbell Occupation: Housework Consort of: Unmarried Informant: N. Wright Relation of Informant: Father	Alice R. Wright, daughter of Nelson Wright

Appendix: Campbell County, Virginia Index of Death Records

Book/Page	Date	Decedent	Information	Identification
	1884/05/09	Stepney C. Wright	Place of Death: Campbell County Race: White Sex: Male Age: 56 Cause: Pneumonia Parents: Ro. & Ellen Wright Born: Campbell Occupation: Farmer Informant: D. E. Ervin Relation of Informant: Physician	Probably 1884 Sterling Charles Wright of Campbell County, son of 1873 Robert D. Wright of Amherst County, grandson of Charles Wright, and probably great grandson of Robert Wright, Sr. (Campbell County)
	1886/09/01	Mary E. Wright	Place of Death: Campbell County Race: White Sex: Female Age: 1 yr & 8 mos Cause: Diphtheria Parents: Tho. & Roberta Wright Born: Campbell County Consort: Unmarried Informant: T. T. Wright Relation of Informant: Father	Mary E. Wright, daughter of Thomas Turner Wright, granddaughter of 1883 Thomas Smith Wright of Campbell County, and great granddaughter of 1842 Thomas Wright of Buckingham County
	1887/01/24	Frank H. Wright	Place of Death: Campbell County Race: White Sex: Male Age: 2 mos Parents: Jno. J. & Susan E. Wright Born: Campbell County Consort of: Unmarried Informant: Jno. J. Wright Relation of Informant: Father	1887 Frank H. Wright of Campbell County, son of John James Wright, grandson of 1883 Thomas Smith Wright of Campbell County, and great grandson of 1842 Thomas Wright of Buckingham County

Appendix: Campbell County, Virginia Index of Death Records

Book/Page	Date	Decedent	Information	Identification
	1887/12/11	Betsy Wright	Place of Death: Campbell County Race: White Sex: Female Age: 70 Cause: Old age Born: Campbell County Occupation: Housekeeping Consort of: Unmarried Informant: Ro. R. Cardwell Relation of Informant: Friend	
	1888/07/09	Mary E. Wright	Place of Death: Campbell County Race: White Sex: Female Age: 19 Cause: Brain Fever Parents: Jas. J. & Susan Wright Born: Campbell County Occupation: Housework Consort of: Unmarried Informant: J. J. Wright Relation of Informant: Father	Mary E. or A. Wright, daughter of John James Wright, granddaughter of 1883 Thomas Smith Wright of Campbell County, and great granddaughter of 1842 Thomas Wright of Buckingham County
	1891/11/10	Fannie Wright	Place of Death: Campbell County Race: Colored Sex: Female Age: 40 Cause: Grippe Born: Campbell County Occupation: Housework Consort of: Henry Wright Informant: H. Wright Relation of Informant: Husband	

Appendix: Campbell County, Virginia Index of Death Records

Book/Page	Date	Decedent	Information	Identification
	1892/07/05	Mary L. Wright	Place of Death: Campbell County Race: White Sex: Female Age: 2 mos Cause: Colera Infantum Parents: R. J. & Sarah Wright Born: Campbell Informant: B. F. Wright Relation of Informant: Father	Mary L. or E. Wright, daughter of 1916 Benjamin Franklin Wright of Campbell County, granddaughter of 1882 Thomas B. Wright of Campbell County, and great granddaughter of Thomas Wright (Campbell County)
	1893/04/13	Melinda Wright	Place of Death: Campbell County Race: Colored Sex: Female Age: 85 Cause: Old Age Born: Campbell County Consort of: Widow Informant: Beauregard Wright Relation of Informant: Son	
	1893/06/16	Anne E. Wright	Place of Death: Campbell County Race: White Sex: Female Age: 30 Cause: Typhoid Fever Born: Campbell County Occupation: Housework Consort of: Edwd. Wright Informant: E. Wright Relation of Informant: Husband	Anne E. (Melton) Wright, wife of Edward Sylvanus Wright, a son of John H. Wright, grandson of 1882 Thomas B. Wright of Campbell County, and great grandson of Thomas Wright (Campbell County)

Book/Page	Date	Decedent	Information	Identification
	1893/07/24	Ernest A. Wright	Place of Death: Campbell County Race: White Sex: Male Age: 10 mos Place: Campbell County Cause: Diarrhea Parents: Edwd. & Ann Wright Born: Campbell County Consort of: Unmarried Informant: E. Wright Relation of Informant: Father	1893 Ernest A. Wright of Campbell County, son of Edward Sylvanus Wright, grandson of John H. Wright, great grandson of 1882 Thomas B. Wright of Campbell County, and great great grandson of Thomas Wright (Campbell County)
	1896/02/12	Sallie Wright	Place of Death: Near Tyreeanna, Campbell County Race: Colored Sex: Female Age: 6 mos Cause: Brain Fever Parents: B. Wright & Nannie Born: Near Tyreeanna Informant: Nannie Wright Relation of Informant: Mother	
	1896/07/25	Nannie Wright	Place of Death: Near Tyreeanna, Campbell County Race: Colored Sex: Female Age: 2 mos Cause: Brain Fever Parents: B Wright & Nannie Born: Near Tyreeanna Informant: Nannie Wright Relation of Informant: Mother	

Appendix: Campbell County, Virginia Index of Death Records

Book/Page	Date	Decedent	Information	Identification
	1913/11/23	Mary Lucy Wright	County: Campbell County	

County: Campbell County
District: Brookvell
Town: Durmid
Residence in City: 7 Yrs.
Sex: Female
Race: Col
Status: Married
Date of Birth:
Age: 54 Years
Occupation: Domestic
Birthplace: Lynchburg
Father's Name: John Cook
Birthplace: Lynchburg
Mother's Name: Sallie Fields
Birthplace: Campbelle Co.
Informant: Anderson Wright
Address: Durmid
Filed: Nov 24, 1913
Registrar: H C Thurman
Cause: Pneumonia
Signed: H O Plunkett M.D.
Date: _____ 1913
Address: Co__y
Length of Residence:
Buried: White Ros_ Cemetary
Date Buried: Nov 25, 191_
Undertaker: Strange & _____
Address: 905-5th

Appendix: Campbell County, Virginia Index of Death Records

Book/Page	Date	Decedent	Information	Identification

1914/04/17   Jenine Wright

County: Campbell County
District: Rustburg
Residence in City:
Sex: Female
Race: Col.
Status: Single
Date of Birth:
Age: 50 yrs May
Occupation: Housekeeper
Birthplace: Campbell Co Va
Father's Name: Nelson Wright
Birthplace:
Mother's Name: Sarah Poor
Birthplace:
Informant: Willie Vandergrift
Address: Rustburg, Va
Filed: April 22, 1914
Registrar: J. M. Goodman
Cause: Apoplexy
Signed: O. L. Watkins M.D.
Date: April 22, 1914
Address: Rustburg Va
Length of Residence:
Buried: Willie Vandergrift
Date Buried: April 18, 1914
Undertaker: Geo A Coleman
Address: Rustburg Va.

Jenine Wright, daughter of Nelson Wright

Appendix: Campbell County, Virginia Index of Death Records

Book/Page	Date	Decedent	Information	Identification
	1914/12/20	Artie Wright	County: Campbell County Sex: Male Race: Colored Status: Single Date of Birth: 2 16, 1903 Age: 11 yrs Occupation: Birthplace: Montgomery W. Va Father's Name: Ernest Wright Birthplace: West Va Mother's Name: Bomase(?) Straton Birthplace: Virginia Informant: Ernest Wright Address: Amherst Va Filed: Dec 21, 1914 Registrar: N L Bondurant Date: 12 20 1914 Cause: Drowned in Canal Signed:: _____ Don(?) Coroner C.C. M.D. Date: 12-21-14 Address: W Lynchburg Length of Res: Buried: Methodist Cemetery Date of Burial: 12-21-1914 Undertaker: Pa____ Undertaking Co. Address: 1015 5th St.	Artie Wright, son of Ernest Wright

Appendix: Campbell County, Virginia Index of Death Records

Book/Page	Date	Decedent	Information	Identification
	1915/03/08	Neally A. Wright	County: Campbell County	

County: Campbell County
District: Brookville
Residence in City:
Sex: F
Race: Wh.
Status: Widowed
Date of Birth: 1855
Age: 60 yrs 9 mos
Occupation:
Birthplace: Bedford Co. Va
Father's Name: Wm Boswell
Birthplace: Va
Mother's Name: Elizebeth Compton
Birthplace: Bedford Co. Va.
Informant: D J Borwell
Address:
Filed: March 9, 1915
Registrar: H C Thurman
Cause: Carcinoma of bowel
Duration: 2 yrs
Signed: H. P__meau Brown M.D.
Date: Mch 8, 1915
Address: Lynchberg, Va. R1
Length of Res:
Buried: Plesant View in Va
Date Buried: March 9, 1915
Undertaker: N D Duiguid
Address: Lbg Va

Book/Page	Date	Decedent	Information	Identification
	1916/02/09	Emeline Wright	County: Campbell County	

District: Rustburg
Town: Rustburg
Sex: Female
Race: Colored
Status: Married
Date of Birth:
Age: 65 yrs
Occupation: Cook
Birthplace: Bunker Hill Bedford County Va.
Father's Name: Unknown
Birthplace:
Mother's Name: Rachel Fuqua
Birthplace:
Informant: Heywood Wright
Address: Rustburg Va
Filed: March 28, 1916
Registrar: J. M. Goodman
Cause: Myocarditis
Contributory: Acute Nephritis
 Parenchymatosis
Signed: O. L. Watkins M.D.
Date: Feb 10, 1916
Address: Rustburg Va
Length of Res:
Buried: Lynchburg Col Cemetery _
Date Buried: Feby 10th 1916
Undertaker: Geo A Coleman
Address: Rustburg Va Sold coffin only

Appendix: Campbell County, Virginia Index of Death Records

Book/Page	Date	Decedent	Information	Identification
	1916/03/07	Benj Franklin Wright	County: Campbell County	1916 Benjamin Franklin Wright of Campbell County, son of 1882 Thomas B. Wright of Campbell County and grandson of Thomas Wright (Campbell County)

County: Campbell County
Sex: M
Race: W
Status: Married
Date of Birth: Apr 25, 1854
Age: 61 yrs
Occupation: Carpanter
Birthplace: Campbell Co Va
Father's Name: Wm Thos Wright
Birthplace: Glouster Co Va
Mother's Name: Sarah _ood(?)
Birthplace: Va
Informant: Sarah F Wright
Address: Durmid Va
Filed: March 7th 1916
Registrar: N. L. Bondurant
Cause: Cerebal Appoplexy
Duration: Eleven Days
Signed: W. Plunkett M.D.
Date: 3/7, 1916
Address: City
Length of Res:
Buried: Presbyterian
Date Buried: Mar 8, 1916
Undertaker: N D Duiguid
Address: Lbg Va

Appendix: Campbell County, Virginia Index of Death Records

Book/Page	Date	Decedent	Information	Identification
	1917/01/14	Minnie Wright	County: Campbell County District: Otter River Town: Altavista Va Sex: Fe Race: W Status: Single Date of Birth: Nov 8/15 Age: 1 yr 2 mos 6 ds Occupation: None Birthplace: Altavista Va Father's Name: S G Wright Birthplace: Syricuse(?) Co NC Mother's Name: Rease(?) Birthplace: Syricuse(?) Co NC Informant: Address: Filed: Jan 15, 1917 Registrar: Cause: Broncho Pneumonia Duration: 6 ds Signed: J Arnold Board M.D. Date: 1-17 1917 Address: Altavista Va Length of Residence: Buried: Altavista Date Buried: Jan 16, 1917 Undertaker: J T Fence Address: Hurt Va	Minnie Wright, daughter of S. G. Wright

Appendix: Campbell County, Virginia Index of Death Records

Book/Page	Date	Decedent	Information	Identification
	1917/12/16	Lucey E. Wright	County: Campbell County District: Bookville Residence: No 204 Shatner St Sex: F5 Race: W Status: Widow Date of Birth: Age: 51 yrs Occupation: Birthplace: Lynchburg Va Father's Name: Benj Milstead Birthplace: Va Mother's Name: Birthplace: Informant: R N Clements Address: N Lbg Va Filed: Dec 17, 1917 Registrar: Floyd Robertson Cause: Paralyssis Duration: 2 yrs. Length of Residence: Buried: Spring Hill Date Buried: Dec 17, 1917 Undertaker: N D Duiguid Address: Lbg Va	Lucy Allen (Milstead) Wright, wife of 1889 George Floyd Wright, a son of George Alexander Wright, grandson of 1823 George Wright of Campbell County, and great grandson of Robert Wright, Sr., (Campbell County)

Appendix: Campbell County, Virginia Index of Death Records

<u>Book/Page</u>	<u>Date</u>	<u>Decedent</u>	<u>Information</u>	<u>Identification</u>
	1918/01/13	Donal Wright	County: Campbell County	Donal Wright, son of A. G. or F. Wright

County: Campbell County
District: Brookville
Sex: M
Race: Colored
Status: Single
Date of Birth: Aug 27, 1891
Age:
Occupation:
Birthplace: Campbell Co.
Father's Name: A. G. Wright
Birthplace: Appomatox
Mother's Name: Lucile Branch
Birthplace: Appomatox
Informant: A. F. Wright
Address: Rout 3 Box 22
Filed: Jan 13, 1918
Registrar: Albert Elliott
Cause: Tuberculosis of Lungs
Duration: 5 mos
Signed: E F Younger M.D.
Date: 1/14, 1918
Address: Lybg. Va
Length of Residence:
Buried: Miggison Cemetery
Date Buried: Jan 15, 1918
Undertaker: W. D. Drugival
Address: 616 Main St

Appendix: Campbell County, Virginia Index of Death Records

Book/Page	Date	Decedent	Information	Identification
	1918/12/28	Charles Henry Wright	County: Campbell County District: Brookville Sex: Male Race: White Status: Single Date of Birth: Mar 16, 1896 Age: 22 yrs 9 mos 12 ds Occupation: Shoe Maker, Craddock Shoe Co Birthplace: Va Father's Name: Benj F. Wright Birthplace: Va Mother's Name: Sarrah F Trent Birthplace: Va Informant: Wm Thos. Wright Address: 603 Maple St. Filed: Dec 28, 1918 Registrar: Floyd Robertson Cause: Pulmonary tuberculosis Duration: 5 mos. Signed: Geo. M. Preston, M.D. Date: Jan 28, 1918 Address: Lynchburg Va. Length of Residence: Buried: Presbyterian Date Buried: Dec 29, 1918 Undertaker: J E. ____ Co Address: 706 Main st	1918 Charles Henry Wright of Campbell County, son of 1916 Benjamin Franklin Wright of Campbell County, grandson of 1882 Thomas B. Wright of Campbell County, and great grandson of Thomas Wright (Campbell County)

Appendix: Campbell County, Virginia Index of Death Records

Book/Page	Date	Decedent	Information	Identification
	1919/01/09	Doyl Wright	County: Campbell County District: Rustburg Sex: Male Race: White Status: Single Date of Birth: November 1909 Age: 10 years 2 months Occupation: None Birthplace: Campbell Father's Name: W. P. Wright Birthplace: Campbell Mother's Name: Sallie Tweedy Birthplace: Campbell Informant: A. H. Tweedy Address: Rustburg Va. Filed: Feb 10, 1919 Registrar: J E Carwile Cause: Pneumonia Contributory Influenza Signed: Col. ____ Date: Jan 23, 1919 Address: Rustburg Va Length of Residence: Buried: New Chappel Date Buried: Jan 10, 1919 Undertaker: E. W. Flynn Address: Gladys Va.	1919 Doyle Patterson Wright of Campbell County, son of 1967 Walter Patterson of Campbell County, grandson of Thomas Turner Wright, great grandson of 1883 Thomas Smith Wright of Campbell County, and great great grandson of 1842 Thomas Wright of Buckingham County

Appendix: Campbell County, Virginia Index of Death Records

Book/Page	Date	Decedent	Information	Identification
	1919/10/30	Mrs. Jennie Wright		

County: Campbell County
District: Rustberg
Residence: No. Campbell Co. Va
Sex: Female
Race: White
Status: Widow
Spouse: David Wright
Date of Birth: July 8, 1851
Age: 68 years 8 months 21 days
Occupation: none
Birthplace: Campbell Co Va
Father's Name: Jas W Pettigrew
Birthplace: Rockbridge Co Va
Mother's Name: Mary Newel
Birthplace: Botetourt Co Va
Informant: A W Lucado (nephew)
Address: 400 Church St Lynchburg Va
Filed: Nov 3 1919
Registrar: John J. Rucker
Cause: Chronic Entero-Colitis
Operation? No
Autopsy? No
Signed: W. Lyle Ould M.D.
Date: Oct 30, 1919
Address: Concord Depot Va
Buried: Family Burial Grounds
Date Buried: 10/31/19
Undertaker: W. D. Duiguid
Address: Lynchburg Va

Mary Virginia (Pettigrew) Wright, wife of David Luther Wright, a son of 1873 John Patterson Wright of Campbell County, grandson of 1811 John Wright of Campbell County, and great grandson of Robert Wright, Sr., (Campbell County)

Appendix: Campbell County, Virginia Index of Death Records

Book/Page	Date	Decedent	Information	Identification
	1920/04/01	Lockey Ann Wright	County: Campbell County District: Seneca City: Gladys Va Residence: Sex: Female Race: White Status: widowed Spouse: Date of Birth: 1828 Age: 92 years Occupation: None Birthplace: Father's Name: Reuben Mitchel Birthplace: Virginia Mother's Name: Kate ____ Birthplace: Virginia Informant: A R Wright Address: Gladys, Va Filed: Apr 30 1920 Registrar: C A Tanner Cause: Natural Causes Contributory: Infirmaties Operation? No Autopsy? No Test confirming diagnosis? None Signed: ____ M.D. Date: 4/3 1920 Address: Gladys Buried: Halifax Co., Va Date Buried: 4-2 1920 Undertaker: E. W. Flynn Address: Gladys Va.	Lockey Ann (Wilson) Wright, wife of James D. Wright, a son of Robert Wright, Jr., and grandson of Robert Wright, Sr., (Campbell County)

Appendix: Campbell County, Virginia Index of Death Records

<u>Book/Page</u>	<u>Date</u>	<u>Decedent</u>	<u>Information</u>	<u>Identification</u>
	1920/09/29	Bettie Wright	County: Campbell County District: Brockville Residence: R. 1. Richmond St Va Sex: Female Race: Colored Status: Spouse: Date of Birth: May 4, 1920 Age: 3 months Occupation: Birthplace: Campbell Co Va Father's Name: Charly Wright Birthplace: Campbell Co Va Mother's Name: Betsy Randalph Birthplace: Campbell Co Va Informant: Charles Wright Address: Lynchberg Va Filed: Sep 29, 1920 Registrar: Floyd Robertson Cause: Whooping Cough Duration: 1 mos Contributory: Pyelitis Duration: 7 ds Operation? No Autopsy? No Test confirming diagnosis? cinical Signed: H P Brown M.D. Date: 9/29, 1920 Address: Lynchburg Va __ Buried: Date Buried: Sept 29, 1920 Undertaker: Address:	Bettie Wright, daughter of Charles Wright

Book/Page	Date	Decedent	Information	Identification
	1930/03/20	Sallie S. Enoch	Place of Death: Campbell County Lynchburg 115 Euclid Ave Residence: 115 Euclid Ave Sex: Female Race: White Status: Married Spouse: George W. Enoch Date of Birth: Oct 23rd 1856 Age: 73 Years 4 Months 25 Days Occupation: At Home Industry: Date last worked: Time spent in occupation: Birthplace: Buckingham Co., Va Father's Name: David Wright Birthplace: Buckingham Co., Va Mother's Name: Mary Ann Wright Birthplace: Buckingham Co., Va Informant: C. A. Enoch Address: Lynchburg, Va. Length of Residence: Buried: Spring Hill, Lynchburg, Va Date Buried: 3/21/30 Undertaker: W. D. Diuguid, Inc. Address: Lynchburg Va. Filed: Mar 21, 1930 Registrar: Grade Cavidson Cause: Cancer of ____ Date of onset: Decr Contributory: old age Name of Operation: none Disease or injury related to occupation? no Signed: W C Rosser, M.D. Address: Lynchburg Va	Sallie S. (Wright) Enoch, daughter of David Wright, granddaughter of 1858 David M. Wright, Jr., and great granddaughter of David M. Wright, Sr., (Buckingham County)

WRIGHT FAMILY

CEMETERY RECORDS BY CEMETERY

CAMPBELL COUNTY, VIRGINIA

Revised as of October 3, 2004

Introduction To Appendix: Cemetery Records, Campbell County, Virginia

This document is an appendix to a larger work titled <u>Sorting Some Of The Wrights Of Southern Virginia</u>. The work is divided into parts for each family of Wrights that has been researched. Each part is divided into two sections; the first section is text discussing the family and the evidence supporting the relationships and the second section is a descendants chart summarizing the relationships and information known about each individual.

The appendices to the work (of which this document is one) present source records for persons named Wright by county and by type of record with the identification of the person named and their Wright ancestors to the extent known.

The source for the records listed in this appendix is the following:

1) Campbell County, Virginia, Family Cemeteries, Volumes I to X, published by the Campbell County Historical Society, 1997 to 2002.

2) Campbell County, Virginia, Church Cemeteries, Volumes I to X, published by the Campbell County Historical Society, 1997 to 2002.

3) Campbell County, Virginia, Public Cemeteries, Volumes I to III, published by the Campbell County Historical Society, 1997 to 1999.

The identification of a person or their ancestor by year and county indicates their year of death and county of residence at death. For example, "1763 Thomas Wright of Bedford County" indicates that this was the Thomas Wright who died in 1763 in Bedford County. If no state is listed after the county, the state is Virginia; counties in states other than Virginia will have a state listed after the county, as in "1876 William S. Wright of Highland County, Ohio".

A parenthetical after the name indicates an identification of the person when a place of death is not yet known, as in "John Wright (Goochland County Carpenter)". A county in parentheses after the name indicates the county with which that person was most identified when no evidence of the place of death has yet been found, as in "Grief Wright (Bedford County)".

All or portions of the text and descendants charts for each Wright family identified are available from the author:

Robert N. Grant
15 Campo Bello Court
Menlo Park, California 94025

(H) 650-854-0895
(O) 650-614-3800

This is a work in process and I would be most interested in receiving additional information about any of the persons identified in these records in order to correct any errors or expand on the information given.

Appendix: Campbell County, Virginia, Cemetery Records

Name	Birth Date	Death Date	Other Information	Cemetery	Identification
Rosa Creasey Wright	1907/04/16	1985/10/31		Altavista Memorial Park Route 29 N., about 1 mile from first exit to Altavista	
Horace J. Wright	1915/00/00	1988/00/00		Altavista Memorial Park Route 29 N., about 1 mile from first exit to Altavista	
Walter Sherwood Wright	1912/11/15	1993/08/22	U.S. Military, World War II	Bethnay United Methodist Church Cemetery Route 663 about 2 miles from Route 615	1993 Walter Sherwood Wright of Campbell County, son of 1967 Walter Patterson Wright of Campbell County, grandson of 1929 Thomas Turner Wright of Campbell County, great grandson of 1883 Thomas Smith Wright of Campbell County, and great great grandson of 1842 Thomas Wright of Buckingham County
Joseph Turner Wright	1963/08/27	1963/08/28		Bethnay United Methodist Church Cemetery Route 663 about 2 miles from Route 615	
Roberta H. Wright	1857/00/00	1934/00/00		Bethnay United Methodist Church Cemetery Route 663 about 2 miles from Route 615	Roberta W. or H. (_____) Wright, wife of 1929 Thomas Turner Wright of Campbell County, a son of 1883 Thomas Smith Wright of Campbell County and grandson of 1842 Thomas Wright of Buckingham County
Thomas T. Wright	1851/00/00	1929/00/00		Bethnay United Methodist Church Cemetery Route 663 about 2 miles from Route 615	1929 Thomas Turner Wright of Campbell County, son of 1883 Thomas Smith Wright of Campbell County and grandson of 1842 Thomas Wright of Buckingham County
John Thomas Wright	1884/02/05	1963/07/24		Candler Family Cemetery West side of Hydaway Road, Route 677, 0.9 miles north of intersection with Route 670 and 2.1 miles south of Route 664	1963 John Thomas Wright of Campbell County, son of James Robert Wright of Campbell County, grandson of 1882 Thomas B. Wright of Campbell County, and great grandson of Thomas Wright (Campbell County)

Appendix: Campbell County, Virginia, Cemetery Records

Name	Birth Date	Death Date	Other Information	Cemetery	Identification
Sarah E. Wright	1872/03/01	1949/03/28		Candler Family Cemetery West side of Hydaway Road, Route 677, 0.9 miles north of intersection with Route 670 and 2.1 miles south of Route 664	Sarah E. (____) Wright, wife of 1960 Waddie B. Wright of Campbell County
Waddie B. Wright	1870/10/08	1960/01/22		Candler Family Cemetery West side of Hydaway Road, Route 677, 0.9 miles north of intersection with Route 670 and 2.1 miles south of Route 664	1960 Waddie B. Wright of Campbell County
Mary Candler Wright	1887/11/22	1955/08/16	Wife of John T. Wright	Candler Family Cemetery West side of Hydaway Road, Route 677, 0.9 miles north of intersection with Route 670 and 2.1 miles south of Route 664	Mary Allen (Candler) Wright, wife of 1963 John Thomas Wright of Campbell County, a son of James Robert Wright of Campbell County, grandson of 1882 Thomas B. Wright of Campbell County, and great grandson of Thomas Wright (Campbell County)
Margaret C. Wright	1919/08/15	1991/12/25	Wife of Leslie N. Wright, Sr.	Candler Family Cemetery West side of Hydaway Road, Route 677, 0.9 miles north of intersection with Route 670 and 2.1 miles south of Route 664	1986 Leslie Nowlin Wright, Sr., of Lynchburg, son of 1963 John Thomas Wright of Campbell County, grandson of James Robert Wright of Campbell County, great grandson of 1882 Thomas B. Wright of Campbell County, and great great grandson of Thomas Wright (Campbell County)
____ Wright	1927/00/00	1927/00/00	Son of James T. Wright per 1927 survey	Candler Family Cemetery West side of Hydaway Road, Route 677, 0.9 miles north of intersection with Route 670 and 2.1 miles south of Route 664	____ Wright, son of James T. Wright

Appendix: Campbell County, Virginia, Cemetery Records

Name	Birth Date	Death Date	Other Information	Cemetery	Identification
____ Wright	0000/00/00	0000/00/00	Child of John Wright who died in 1925 per 1927 survey	Candler Family Cemetery West side of Hydaway Road, Route 677, 0.9 miles north of intersection with Route 670 and 2.1 miles south of Route 664	____ Wright, child of 1925 John Wright
Lessie V. Wright	1925/03/28	1997/01/24	Wife of Edell L. Wright	Candler Family Cemetery West side of Hydaway Road, Route 677, 0.9 miles north of intersection with Route 670 and 2.1 miles south of Route 664	Lessie Virginia (Evans) Wright, wife of Edell Lee Wright, a son of 1963 John Thomas Wright of Campbell County, grandson of James Robert Wright, Sr., of Campbell County, great grandson of 1882 Thomas B. Wright of Campbell County, and great great grandson of Thomas Wright (Campbell County)
Clara Lucille Wright	1914/03/00	1914/03/00	Infant of James R. and Carrie Candler Wright per FF #3795	Candler Family Cemetery West side of Hydaway Road, Route 677, 0.9 miles north of intersection with Route 670 and 2.1 miles south of Route 664	Clara Lucille Wright, daughter of 1978 James Robert Wright, Jr., of Campbell County, granddaughter of James Robert Wright, Sr., of Campbell County, great granddaughter of 1882 Thomas B. Wright of Campbell County, and great great granddaughter of Thomas Wright (Campbell County)
Mary H. Wright	1909/03/15	1981/10/27		Concord Cemetery Concord, Virginia	
Lona G. Wright	1890/08/09	1952/09/19		Ebenezer Baptist Church Cemetery, Ebenezer Road, Naruna, Brookneal quadrant	
Gordon Wright	1926/12/30	1972/12/09		Ebenezer Baptist Church Cemetery, Ebenezer Road, Naruna, Brookneal quadrant	
Sue Toler Wright	1903/05/07	1996/02/05	Wife of William E. Wright	Ebenezer Baptist Church Cemetery, Ebenezer Road, Naruna, Brookneal quadrant	

Appendix: Campbell County, Virginia, Cemetery Records

Name	Birth Date	Death Date	Other Information	Cemetery	Identification
William Edward Wright	1889/03/23	1962/05/17		Ebenezer Baptist Church Cemetery, Ebenezer Road, Naruna, Brookneal quadrant	
Lucy Ann Wright	1885/01/14	1968/04/12		Ebenezer Baptist Church Cemetery, Ebenezer Road, Naruna, Brookneal quadrant	
Norman Oliver Wright	1893/03/25	1950/10/30		Ebenezer Baptist Church Cemetery, Ebenezer Road, Naruna, Brookneal quadrant	
Dorine Davis Wright	1897/03/02	1983/08/18		Ebenezer Baptist Church Cemetery, Ebenezer Road, Naruna, Brookneal quadrant	
Charles Henry Wright	1862/04/17	1941/08/14		Ebenezer Baptist Church Cemetery, Ebenezer Road, Naruna, Brookneal quadrant	
Eliza Ann Cardwell Wright	1862/08/05	1944/02/02		Ebenezer Baptist Church Cemetery, Ebenezer Road, Naruna, Brookneal quadrant	
Carter Henry Wright	1920/12/31	1978/07/04	SN, U.S. Navy	Ebenezer Baptist Church Cemetery, Ebenezer Road, Naruna, Brookneal quadrant	
Alva R. Wright	1886/10/28	1959/12/09		Ebenezer Baptist Church Cemetery, Ebenezer Road, Naruna, Brookneal quadrant	

Appendix: Campbell County, Virginia, Cemetery Records

Name	Birth Date	Death Date	Other Information	Cemetery	Identification
Monica Riley Wright	1971/01/25	1998/04/14		First Baptist Church Cemetery Evington on Route 683 about 1½ miles from Route 24 in Lynch Station qudrant	
Jesse Edwin Wright	1878/00/00	1902/00/00		Gough Family Cemetery 1/4 mile due west from First St. Paul's Baptist Church, Woodbridge Road, Route 501	Jesse Edwin Wright, son of 1881 Jesse Hughes or Hubert Wright of Campbell County, grandson of 1873 John Patterson Wright of Campbell County, great grandson of 1811 John Wright of Campbell County, and great great grandson of Robert Wright, Sr., (Campbell County)
David Stephen Wright	1952/09/17	1952/11/28		Kedron Baptist Church Cemetery Near center of Campbell County on east side of Route 501	
Randolph Torian Wright, Sr.	1923/07/31	1965/05/15	Va MOMM3, USNR, World War II	Kedron Baptist Church Cemetery Near center of Campbell County on east side of Route 501	
Grover H. Wright	1922/07/06	1991/03/09	Pfc. U.S. Army, World War II	Lambs United Methodist Church, Route 701 approx. 1.08 miles from Route 699 & 2.50 miles from Route 686	

Appendix: Campbell County, Virginia, Cemetery Records

Name	Birth Date	Death Date	Other Information	Cemetery	Identification
Charlie Wright	0000/00/00	1932/08/23		Lawyers Missionary Baptist Church Cemetery North side of Waterlick Road (Route 622), ¼ mile from intersection of Waterlick & Lawyers Rd.	
Charlie W. Wright	1934/02/05	1966/09/12		Lawyers Missionary Baptist Church Cemetery North side of Waterlick Road (Route 622), ¼ mile from intersection of Waterlick & Lawyers Rd.	
Charlie R. Wright	1907/02/27	1941/09/24		Lawyers Missionary Baptist Church Cemetery North side of Waterlick Road (Route 622), ¼ mile from intersection of Waterlick & Lawyers Rd.	
Jesse H. Wright	1854/09/13	1881/05/14		Mt. Vernon Baptist Church Cemetery, Route 656 near Route 24 in Rustburg quadrant	1881 Jesse Hughes or Hubert Wright of Campbell County, son of 1873 John Patterson Wright of Campbell County, grandson of 1811 John Wright of Campbell County, and great grandson of Robert Wright, Sr., (Campbell County)
Elizabeth H. Wright	1814/00/00	1886/00/00	Whitten Funeral Home Marker	Mt. Vernon Baptist Church Cemetery, Route 656 near Route 24 in Rustburg quadrant	Martha Elizabeth (Hughes) Wright, wife of 1873 John Patterson Wright of Campbell County, a son of 1811 John Wright of Campbell County and grandson of Robert Wright, Sr., (Campbell County)
John P. Wright	1808/00/00	1878/00/00	Whitten Funeral Home Marker	Mt. Vernon Baptist Church Cemetery, Route 656 near Route 24 in Rustburg quadrant	1873 John Patterson Wright of Campbell County, son of 1811 John Wright of Campbell County and grandson of Robert Wright, Sr., (Campbell County)

Appendix: Campbell County, Virginia, Cemetery Records

Name	Birth Date	Death Date	Other Information	Cemetery	Identification
Rhonda S. Wright	1962/07/16	1994/07/06		Mt. Zion United Methodist Church Red House Road, Route 615 in Gladys quadrant	
Gary Wayne Wright	1950/11/05	1969/05/03	Va. Sp 4, Co. B, 2nd Bn., 503 Inv., Viet Nam, BSM-PH	New Prospect Baptist Church Cemetery Prospect Road, Hurt	
John Boone Wright, Jr.	1919/08/09	1975/10/30	Pfc. Army Air Force, World War II	New Prospect Baptist Church Cemetery Prospect Road, Hurt	
Mary McFaden Wright	1884/09/04	1961/08/22	Wife of Levi G. Wright	Penuel Baptist Church Cemetery, Route 29 and Penuel Road, Castle Craig quadrant of Campbell Co.	
Jasper J. Wright	1911/11/23	1945/03/24		Pleasant View Baptist Church Cemetery 0.15 miles west of Campbell County line, northwest side of Route 221, Lynchburg, formerly Bedford County	
Virginia F. Wright	1882/03/23	1967/02/24		Pleasant View Baptist Church Cemetery 0.15 miles west of Campbell County line, northwest side of Route 221, Lynchburg, formerly Bedford County	Virginia F. Wright, daughter of 1909 James K. Wright of Bedford County, granddaughter of 1883 Anslem Wright of Franklin County, and great granddaughter of William Wright (Franklin County)

Appendix: Campbell County, Virginia, Cemetery Records

Name	Birth Date	Death Date	Other Information	Cemetery	Identification
Mollie A. Boswell Wright	1854/05/19	1915/03/08		Pleasant View Baptist Church Cemetery 0.15 miles west of Campbell County line, northwest side of Route 221, Lynchburg, formerly Bedford County	Mary Ann (Boswell) Wright, wife of 1909 James K. Wright of Bedford County, a son of 1883 Anslem Wright of Franklin County and grandson of William Wright (Franklin County)
Margaret L. Wright	1921/06/13	1940/11/23		Pleasant View Baptist Church Cemetery 0.15 miles west of Campbell County line, northwest side of Route 221, Lynchburg, formerly Bedford County	
Samuel J. Wright	1883/06/22	1969/02/10		Pleasant View Baptist Church Cemetery 0.15 miles west of Campbell County line, northwest side of Route 221, Lynchburg, formerly Bedford County	1969 Samuel J. Wright of Campbell County, son of 1909 James K. Wright of Bedford County, grandson of 1883 Anslem Wright of Franklin County, and great grandson of William Wright (Franklin County)
Bertha Kersey Wright	1885/10/02	1963/03/04		Pleasant View Baptist Church Cemetery 0.15 miles west of Campbell County line, northwest side of Route 221, Lynchburg, formerly Bedford County	
James A. Wright	1879/09/22	1928/12/18		Pleasant View Baptist Church Cemetery 0.15 miles west of Campbell County line, northwest side of Route 221, Lynchburg, formerly Bedford County	1928 James A. Wright of Bedford County, son of 1909 James K. Wright of Bedford County, grandson of 1883 Anslem Wright of Franklin County, and great grandson of William Wright (Franklin County)

Appendix: Campbell County, Virginia, Cemetery Records

Name	Birth Date	Death Date	Other Information	Cemetery	Identification
Louis Marvin Wright	1907/12/26	1921/05/20		Pleasant View Baptist Church Cemetery 0.15 miles west of Campbell County line, northwest side of Route 221, Lynchburg, formerly Bedford County	
Lillie W. Wright	1879/10/20	1918/02/27	Wife of James A. Wright	Pleasant View Baptist Church Cemetery 0.15 miles west of Campbell County line, northwest side of Route 221, Lynchburg, formerly Bedford County	Lillie W. (____) Wright, wife of 1928 James A. Wright of Bedford County, a son of 1909 James K. Wright of Bedford County, grandson of 1883 Anslem Wright of Franklin County, and great grandson of William Wright (Franklin County)
Julian Morton Wright	0000/00/00	1928/04/08	Va. Sgt., 38th Inf., World War I	Pleasant View Baptist Church Cemetery 0.15 miles west of Campbell County line, northwest side of Route 221, Lynchburg, formerly Bedford County	1928 Julian Morton Wright of Campbell County, son of Oliver T. Wright, grandson of 1883 Anslem Wright of Franklin County, and grandson of William Wright (Franklin County)
Hollis R. "Bob" Wright	1917/06/14	1971/11/16		Pleasant View Baptist Church Cemetery 0.15 miles west of Campbell County line, northwest side of Route 221, Lynchburg, formerly Bedford County	
James K. Wright	1843/03/13	1909/11/05		Pleasant View Baptist Church Cemetery 0.15 miles west of Campbell County line, northwest side of Route 221, Lynchburg, formerly Bedford County	1909 James K. Wright of Bedford County, son of 1883 Anslem Wright of Franklin County and grandson of William Wright (Franklin County)

Appendix: Campbell County, Virginia, Cemetery Records

Name	Birth Date	Death Date	Other Information	Cemetery	Identification
Eldridge J. Wright	1906/12/02	1936/12/13		Pleasant View Baptist Church Cemetery 0.15 miles west of Campbell County line, northwest side of Route 221, Lynchburg, formerly Bedford County	
Harold S. Wright, Jr.	1952/05/29	1952/08/09		Pleasant View Baptist Church Cemetery 0.15 miles west of Campbell County line, northwest side of Route 221, Lynchburg, formerly Bedford County	
Thomas W. Wright	1885/07/12	1924/08/31		Sharon United Methodist Church Cemetery Long Island quadrant of Campbell Co. Va.	
Edna V. Wright	1910/01/29	1999/12/20		Shiloh United Methodist Church Intersection of Forest Road & Graves Mill Road in Lynchburg quadrant	
Nellie Elizabeth Wright	1931/07/20	1965/11/17		Shiloh United Methodist Church Intersection of Forest Road & Graves Mill Road in Lynchburg quadrant	
Nellie Conner Wright	1907/00/00	1935/00/00		Shiloh United Methodist Church Intersection of Forest Road & Graves Mill Road in Lynchburg quadrant	

Appendix: Campbell County, Virginia, Cemetery Records

Name	Birth Date	Death Date	Other Information	Cemetery	Identification
John William Wright	1880/06/10	1928/01/31		Shiloh United Methodist Church Intersection of Forest Road & Graves Mill Road in Lynchburg quadrant	
W. T. Wright	1837/03/25	1927/01/14		Shiloh United Methodist Church Intersection of Forest Road & Graves Mill Road in Lynchburg quadrant	
Ruth A. Bond Wright	1855/10/31	1934/03/07	Wife of W. T. Wright	Shiloh United Methodist Church Intersection of Forest Road & Graves Mill Road in Lynchburg quadrant	
Alice May Booth Wright	1904/05/18	2000/09/13	Wife of Thomas Rasworth Wright	White's United Methodist Church Cemetery Route 738 between Route 622 & Route 29	
Annie Mc. Wright	1903/01/22	1959/12/16		White's United Methodist Church Cemetery Route 738 between Route 622 & Route 29	
Roseworth T. Wright	1924/12/22	1983/06/07		White's United Methodist Church Cemetery Route 738 between Route 622 & Route 29	

Appendix: Campbell County, Virginia, Cemetery Records

Name	Birth Date	Death Date	Other Information	Cemetery	Identification
Gordon M. Wright	1902/06/28	1940/12/11		White's United Methodist Church Cemetery Route 738 between Route 622 & Route 29	
Roy Lester Wright	1904/02/22	1972/11/03		Williamson-Wright Cemetery West side of Route 612 Campbell Co., Va	
Florence Esther Wright	1903/03/26	1971/03/14	Wife of Waddie B. Wright	Williamson-Wright Cemetery West side of Route 612 Campbell Co., Va	Florence Esther (____) Wright, wife of 1960 Waddie B. Wright of Campbell County

INDEX

WRIGHT FAMILY

PROBATE RECORDS

CAMPBELL COUNTY, VIRGINIA

1782 to 1900

Revised as of September 5, 2004

Introduction To Appendix: Probate Records for Campbell County, Virginia

This document is an appendix to a larger work titled Sorting Some Of The Wrights Of Southern Virginia. The work is divided into parts for each family of Wrights that has been researched. Each part is divided into two sections; the first section is text discussing the family and the evidence supporting the relationships and the second section is a descendants chart summarizing the relationships and information known about each individual.

The appendices to the work (of which this document is one) present source records for persons named Wright by county and by type of record with the identification of the person named and their Wright ancestors to the extent known.

The source for the records listed in this appendix is the following:

      Campbell County, Virginia, Probate Records, available from the Clerk of the Circuit Court, P.O. Box 7, Rustburg, Virginia 24588.

The identification of a person or their ancestor by year and county indicates their year of death and county of residence at death. For example, "1763 Thomas Wright of Bedford County" indicates that this was the Thomas Wright who died in 1763 in Bedford County. If no state is listed after the county, the state is Virginia; counties in states other than Virginia will have a state listed after the county, as in "1876 William S. Wright of Highland County, Ohio".

A parenthetical after the name indicates an identification of the person when a place of death is not yet known, as in "John Wright (Goochland County Carpenter)". A county in parentheses after the name indicates the county with which that person was most identified when no evidence of the place of death has yet been found, as in "Grief Wright (Bedford County)".

All or portions of the text and descendants charts for each Wright family identified are available from the author:

      Robert N. Grant
      15 Campo Bello Court   (H) 650-854-0895
      Menlo Park, California 94025   (O) 650-614-3800

This is a work in progress and I would be most interested in receiving additional information about any of the persons identified in these records in order to correct any errors or expand on the information given.

Appendix: Campbell County, Virginia, Probate Records:

Book/Page		Date	Decedent	Document	Identification
02	226	1805/12/09	Thomas Wright	Will	1805 Thomas Wright of Campbell County, son of 1779 John Wright of Prince Edward County
02	265	1806/04/14	Thomas Wright	Appsmt.	1805 Thomas Wright of Campbell County, son of 1779 John Wright of Prince Edward County
02	388	1808/06/01	Thomas Wright	Acct.	1805 Thomas Wright of Campbell County, son of 1779 John Wright of Prince Edward County
04	361	1821/10/08	Robert Wright	Acct.	1818 Robert Wright of Campbell County, son of 1805 Thomas Wright of Campbell County and grandson of 1779 John Wright of Prince Edwards County
04	407	1822/08/12	James T. Wright	Appsmt.	1822 James T. Wright of Campbell County, son of James Wright and grandson of 1779 John Wright of Prince Edward County
04	450	1823/03/10	George Wright	Will	1823 George Wright of Campbell County, son of Robert Wright, Sr. (Campbell County)
04	487	1823/07/14	George Wright	Appsmt.	1823 George Wright of Campbell County, son of Robert Wright, Sr. (Campbell County)
05	040	1823/11/13	James T. Wright	Acct.	1822 James T. Wright of Campbell County, son of James Wright and grandson of 1779 John Wright of Prince Edward County
05	133	1825/01/13	George Wright	Acct.	1823 George Wright of Campbell County, son of Robert Wright, Sr. (Campbell County)
05	277	1826/03/15	Robert Wright	Appsmt.	1818 Robert Wright of Campbell County, son of 1805 Thomas Wright of Campbell County and grandson of 1779 John Wright of Prince Edward County
05	346	1826/08/14	Robert Wright	Acct.	1818 Robert Wright of Campbell County, son of 1805 Thomas Wright of Campbell County and grandson of 1779 John Wright of Prince Edward County
06	348	1829/12/14	Thomas P. Wright Gdn.	Acct.	Thomas Pryor Wright, son of 1818 Robert Wright of Campbell County, grandson of 1805 Thomas Wright of Campbell County and great grandson of 1779 John Wright of Prince Edward County

Appendix: Campbell County, Virginia, Probate Records:

Book/Page		Date	Decedent	Document	Identification
06	462	1830/12/13	Thomas P. Wright Gdn.	Acct.	Thomas Pryor Wright, son of 1818 Robert Wright of Campbell County, grandson of 1805 Thomas Wright of Campbell County and great grandson of 1779 John Wright of Prince Edward County
07	065	1832/01/09	Thomas P. Wright Gdn.	Acct.	Thomas Pryor Wright, son of 1818 Robert Wright of Campbell County, grandson of 1805 Thomas Wright of Campbell County and great grandson of 1779 John Wright of Prince Edward County
07	150	1832/12/10	Thomas P. Wright Gdn.	Acct.	Thomas Pryor Wright, son of 1818 Robert Wright of Campbell County, grandson of 1805 Thomas Wright of Campbell County and great grandson of 1779 John Wright of Prince Edward County
07	234	1833/12/09	Thomas P. Wright Gdn.	Acct	Thomas Pryor Wright, son of 1818 Robert Wright of Campbell County, grandson of 1805 Thomas Wright of Campbell County and great grandson of 1779 John Wright of Prince Edward County
07	325	1835/01/12	Thomas P. Wright Gdn.	Acct.	Thomas Pryor Wright, son of 1818 Robert Wright of Campbell County, grandson of 1805 Thomas Wright of Campbell County and great grandson of 1779 John Wright of Prince Edward County
07	399	1836/01/11	Thomas P. Wright Gdn.	Acct.	Thomas Pryor Wright, son of 1818 Robert Wright of Campbell County, grandson of 1805 Thomas Wright of Campbell County and great grandson of 1779 John Wright of Prince Edward County
08	190	1838/03/12	Sylvia Wright	Appsmt.	Sylvia (____) (____) Wright, non-wife of 1805 Thomas Wright of Campbell County and mother of 1818 Robert Wright of Campbell County
08	267	1839/04/08	Sylvia Wright	Acct.	Sylvia (____) (____) Wright, non-wife of 1805 Thomas Wright of Campbell County and mother of 1818 Robert Wright of Campbell County
11	302	1855/01/08	William Wright	Appsmt. & Sales	1854 William Wright of Campbell County, son of 1814 John Wright of Bedford County and grandson of John Wright (Goochland County Carpenter)
11	462	1856/09/08	William Wright	Acct.	1854 William Wright of Campbell County, son of 1814 John Wright of Bedford County and grandson of John Wright (Goochland County Carpenter)

Appendix: Campbell County, Virginia, Probate Records:

Book/Page		Date	Decedent	Document	Identification
12	066	1858/04/00	William Wright	Acct.	1854 William Wright of Campbell County, son of 1814 John Wright of Bedford County and grandson of John Wright (Goochland County Carpenter)
12	356	1861/04/00	George A. Wright Trust	Acct.	
13	077	1862/11/17	Samuel B. Wright	Apmt.	1862 Samuel B. Wright of Campbell County, son of 1877 James Wright of Augusta County
13	091	1863/03/09	William Wright	Acct.	1854 William Wright of Campbell County, son of 1814 John Wright of Bedford County and grandson of John Wright (Goochland County Carpenter)
14	158	1873/06/00	John P. Wright, Sr.	Will	1873 John Patterson Wright of Campbell County, son of 1811 John Wright of Campbell County and grandson of Robert Wright, Sr. (Campbell County)
14	292	1875/01/11	John P. Wright	Appsmt.	1873 John Patterson Wright of Campbell County, son of 1811 John Wright of Campbell County and grandson of Robert Wright, Sr. (Campbell County)
15	349	1880/10/11	Elijah Wright	Appsmt.	1880 Elijah Wright of Campbell County, son of 1835 Benjamin Wright of Bedford County, grandson of 1814 John Wright of Bedford County, and great grandson of John Wright (Goochland County Carpenter)
16	019	1882/07/13	Elijah Wright	Acct. of Sales	1880 Elijah Wright of Campbell County, son of 1835 Benjamin Wright of Bedford County, grandson of 1814 John Wright of Bedford County, and great grandson of John Wright (Goochland County Carpenter)
16	076	1883/05/00	Thomas S. Wright	Will	1883 Thomas S. Wright of Campbell County, son of 1842 Thomas Wright of Buckingham County
16	266	1885/04/00	John P. Wright	Acct.	1873 John Patterson Wright of Campbell County, son of 1811 John Wright of Campbell County and grandson of Robert Wright, Sr. (Campbell County)
17	095	1891/03/09	Elijah Wright	Acct	1880 Elijah Wright of Campbell County, son of 1835 Benjamin Wright of Bedford County, grandson of 1814 John Wright of Bedford County, and great grandson of John Wright (Goochland County Carpenter)

INDEX

Wright Family Records: Land Tax List, Bedford County, Virginia, 1782-1850

Wright Family Records: Lynchburg, Virginia Birth Records (1853-1896), Marriage Records (1805-1900), Marriage Notices (1794-1880), Census Records (1900), Deed Records (1805-1900), Death Records (1853-1896), Probate Records (1805-1900)

Wright Family Records: Marriages in Bedford County, Virginia

Wright Family Records: Prince Edward County, Virginia Birth Records, Marriage Records, Election Polls, and Tithe List, Personal Property Tax List, Census

0788438107